WHAT DO YOU KNOW ABOUT

DEPRESSION & MENTAL HEALTH

PETE SANDERS and STEVE MYERS

COPPER BEECH BOOKS

BROOKFIELD, CONNECTICUT

An Aladdin Book
© Aladdin Books Ltd 1996
© U.S. text 1998

Designed and produced by
Aladdin Books Ltd
28 Percy Street
London W1P 0LD

First published
in the United States in 1998 by
Copper Beech Books,
an imprint of
The Millbrook Press
2 Old New Milford Road
Brookfield, Connecticut 06804

Printed in Belgium

Design   David West
                  Children's Books
Designer   Robert Perry
Editor   Alex Edmonds
Picture research Brooks Krikler
                  Research
Illustrator   Mike Lacey

**Library of Congress
Cataloging-in-Publication Data**
Sanders, Pete.
Depression and mental health / Pete Sanders
and Steve Myers ; illustrated by Mike Lacey.
p. cm. — (What do you know about)
Includes index.
Summary: Discusses depression and other
aspects of mental health, and the effects such
illnesses can have on the depressed person and
those around him.
ISBN 0-7613-0802-4 (lib. bdg.)
1. Depression, Mental—Juvenile literature.
2. Depression in children—Juvenile literature.
3. Mental health—Juvenile literature.
[1. Depression, Mental. 2. Mental health.]
I. Myers, Steve. II. Lacey, Mike, ill.
III. Title. IV. Series: Sanders, Pete.
What do you know about.
RC537.S364 1998   97-41647
616.85'27—dc21   CIP AC

5 4 3 2 1

CONTENTS

HOW TO USE THIS BOOK
The books in this series are intended to help young people to understand more about issues that may affect their lives.

Each book can be read by a child alone, or together with a parent, teacher, or guardian. Issues raised in the storyline are further discussed in the accompanying text, so that there is an opportunity to talk through ideas as they come up.

At the end of the book there is a section called "What Can We Do?" This gives practical ideas that will be useful for both young people and adults. Organizations and helplines are also listed, to provide the reader with additional sources of information and support.

INTRODUCTION

THOUSANDS OF PEOPLE WORLDWIDE SUFFER FROM DEPRESSION OR SOME FORM OF MENTAL DISTRESS.

However, people are often reluctant to discuss the subject, and this has led to much misunderstanding — even fear — of the issues involved. This book will help you to understand depression and other aspects of mental health, and show how they can affect people's lives. Each chapter introduces a different aspect of the subject, illustrated by a continuing storyline. The characters in the story have to deal with situations which many young people may experience. After each episode we stop and look at the issues raised, and broaden the discussion. By the end you will know more about depression and mental health and the help and support that is available, and understand the importance of taking care of yourself.

EMOTIONAL HEALTH

YOU KNOW HOW IMPORTANT IT IS TO CHOOSE A HEALTHY LIFESTYLE.

However, this doesn't just mean being physically fit and eating the right kinds of food. It also involves taking care of your mental and emotional health.

Experiencing emotional ups and downs is a natural part of life, especially during puberty, when you might go through periods of gloom, followed by times when you feel very happy and optimistic. We all have to deal with different kinds of problems and handle difficult thoughts and feelings. Facing up to these is not always easy. Taking care of yourself emotionally means learning to understand your feelings, where they come from, and how they can be affected by outside influences. Emotional and physical well-being are often connected. If you have a cold, this might make you feel miserable. In the same way, feelings can sometimes affect you physically. For instance, if you are nervous or frightened, you might feel sick, or be suddenly unable to move. Mental and emotional problems and distresses can be just as damaging to people's lives as injury and diseases. This is why it's important to think of the whole person in relation to health issues.

Emotions such as jealousy are often very difficult to deal with.

▽ Trisha La Salle and her younger brother Alan were on their way to school.

WHAT'S THE MATTER WITH YOU? YOU HARDLY SAID A WORD AT BREAKFAST. YOU CAN'T STILL BE UPSET.

WHY NOT? YOU WEREN'T THE ONE WHO HAD TO LISTEN TO MOM LECTURING ME ALL NIGHT ABOUT HOW I COULD DO BETTER IN SCHOOL.

I STILL DON'T SEE WHY YOU'RE IN SUCH A BAD MOOD.

IT'S OKAY FOR YOU. SHE LEAVES YOU ALONE, BUT SHE'S ALWAYS ON MY BACK. IT'S NOT FAIR, WHY ME ALL THE TIME?

▽ Alan's friends were waiting for him to arrive.

▷ Trisha wouldn't discuss it anymore and ran on ahead.

HI. WHAT'S GOING ON? WHO'S THE NEW BOY?

WE DON'T KNOW. HE LOOKS A BIT ODD TO ME, THOUGH. LOOK AT THOSE GLASSES!

HE CAN'T HELP HAVING TO WEAR THEM. LET'S GO AND TALK TO HIM.

YOU'RE NEW HERE, AREN'T YOU? WHAT'S YOUR NAME?

IAN SUMMERS. THIS IS MY FIRST DAY.

HOW COME YOU HAD TO MOVE SCHOOLS HALFWAY THROUGH A SEMESTER?

▽ Ian didn't answer at first. Then he decided he might as well tell them the truth.

MY DAD LOST HIS JOB SIX MONTHS AGO AND COULDN'T FIND WORK. WE HAD TO SELL THE HOUSE AND MOVE.

THAT'S AWFUL. I'M ALAN BY THE WAY. THIS IS DEEPAK AND SLEEPY HERE IS RICKY.

SORRY. I DIDN'T SLEEP MUCH LAST NIGHT. MOM AND DAD WERE ARGUING AGAIN - THEY SEEM TO DO NOTHING BUT SHOUT AT EACH OTHER THESE DAYS. IT'S GETTING RIDICULOUS.

WHO'S ALAN TALKING TO?

I DON'T KNOW. LISA WHAT HAVE YOU GOT ON YOUR FACE? YOUR SKIN'S ORANGE!

NADINE! YOU SAID IT LOOKED OKAY. IT'S A NEW CREAM, TRISHA. IT'S SUPPOSED TO COVER UP MY PIMPLES.

△ Before Trisha could tell her it didn't quite work, the bell went and they hurried into class.

Nobody yet fully understands exactly where feelings come from.
What is known is that the way you feel can be directly influenced both by the way you feel about yourself and the way you are treated by others. Friends, family, other people, your social situation and cultural background, and the decisions you make can all have an effect on your feelings. It may not always be something that happens to you directly that affects you. Someone else's suffering or happiness can also bring out an emotional response.

Trisha is upset about her parents' expectations of her.
A mood is a mixture of emotions that affects how you respond in situations. During puberty mood swings are common. Moods are not usually a problem, unless they become extreme and long-lasting.

Ian is quite shy about talking to the others about his situation.
Not everyone has the same feelings or the same way of showing them. Some can discuss their emotions with their friends or family easily. Others prefer to work them through privately. People often expect you to react in a particular way at certain times. However, the feeling you have may not be the same as theirs. You have to come to terms with your own emotional situation, and find your own way of expressing emotions appropriately and healthily.

WHAT IS DEPRESSION?

DEPRESSION IS A STRONG MOOD OF SADNESS OR DESPAIR, WHICH CAN INFLUENCE HOW YOU FEEL ABOUT PEOPLE AND SITUATIONS.

For instance, if you think something is unfair or hopeless, or if you have argued with a good friend, you might feel "down" about it. Most of these kinds of depressive episodes will stop in a relatively short time. For some people depression goes beyond the mild negative feelings we all experience. For them, the depression becomes very intense and long-lasting. Each individual case will be different, but most incidents of serious depression begin with an initial downward mood swing, which becomes more and more severe. People might be overcome by a feeling of total despair. As the depression gets worse, they will have increasingly negative emotions – perhaps feeling worthless and a disappointment to everybody.

People who are depressed often feel they have no energy and no will to do anything.

▽A few days later, Ian's mom asked how he was settling in at school.

OKAY, I SUPPOSE. THERE'S THIS ONE GUY - DANNY - WHO'S A REAL PAIN, BUT I'VE MADE A COUPLE OF FRIENDS. I REALLY MISS MY OLD SCHOOL, THOUGH.

NOT AGAIN! THAT'S ALL HE DOES THESE DAYS. HE'S NOT EVEN TRYING TO GET A JOB ANYMORE. HE JUST SLEEPS, OR SITS AROUND STARING AT THE TV.

I KNOW, DARLING. TURN THE RADIO DOWN A BIT WOULD YOU? YOUR DAD'S STILL SLEEPING.

THAT'S NOT TRUE, IAN. YOUR DAD'S VERY UPSET BY ALL THIS. IT'S AFFECTED HIM BADLY.

WHAT ABOUT US? HE DOESN'T SEEM TO CARE ANYMORE. ALL THIS IS HIS FAULT IN THE FIRST PLACE.

IAN THAT'S A HORRIBLE THING TO SAY!

▽His mom was startled by a voice from the hallway.

SOMETIMES, I THINK HE'S RIGHT. YOU'D PROBABLY BOTH BE BETTER OFF WITHOUT ME.

△Ian just grabbed his schoolbag and stormed out of the house.

LONG ENOUGH. DO YOU FEEL THE SAME WAY? LIKE THIS IS ALL MY FAULT?

JOHN, YOU MADE ME JUMP. HOW LONG HAVE YOU BEEN STANDING THERE?

BECAUSE I DON'T NEED A DOCTOR. AND I ESPECIALLY DON'T NEED TO SEE YOUR BROTHER, THE PSYCHIATRIST.

OF COURSE NOT JOHN, I'M REALLY WORRIED ABOUT YOU. YOU'VE NOT BEEN YOURSELF LATELY. WHY WON'T YOU LET ME CALL MAX?

△Mrs. Summers tried to talk to him, but he turned away and went into the living room.

▽ A few weeks later, after school, Alan asked who wanted to go into town.

I'LL GO. I'M IN NO HURRY TO GET HOME. IT'S LIKE A WAR ZONE THERE AT THE MOMENT.

DO THEY EVER NOT FIGHT? HEY, LET'S GO TO MARIO'S FOR A PIZZA.

GREAT IDEA. I LOVE PIZZA.

THAT'S BECAUSE IT MATCHES YOUR FACE!

SHUT UP, YOU LITTLE SQUIRT!

ALAN, LEAVE HER ALONE. SHE CAN'T HELP HER PIMPLES.

MY SISTER HAD THE WORST ACNE WHEN SHE WAS YOUR AGE. IT MADE HER REALLY MISERABLE.

DO YOU MIND! IT'S BAD ENOUGH, WITHOUT EVERYONE DRAWING ATTENTION TO IT ALL THE TIME.

I WOULDN'T WORRY. PIMPLES ARE JUST PART OF GROWING UP - LIKE SCHOOL AND EXAMS.

PLEASE DON'T MENTION EXAMS! MOM'S ON MY BACK AGAIN ABOUT HOW IMPORTANT IT IS TO DO WELL.

I TRY MY BEST, BUT IT'S LIKE NOTHING IS EVER GOOD ENOUGH. THEY CRITICIZE EVERYTHING. EVEN WHEN I DO GET A GOOD GRADE, THEY ALWAYS TELL ME IT COULD BE BETTER.

MINE TOO. MOST OF THE TIME I TRY TO IGNORE HER.

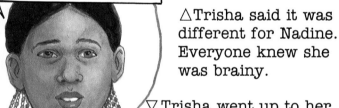

▽ The following evening, Trisha was watching TV.

△Trisha said it was different for Nadine. Everyone knew she was brainy.

▽ Trisha went up to her room. An hour later, Alan and Ricky looked in.

TRISHA HAVE YOU FINISHED YOUR HOMEWORK? YOU KNOW HOW IMPORTANT YOUR GRADES ARE.

I KNOW MOM. YOU NEVER STOP TELLING ME. I FINISHED AGES AGO.

WHAT'S GOING ON? MOM AND DAD ARE IN A REAL MOOD.

TRISHA DID YOU EAT ALL THOSE BY YOURSELF? YOU'LL GET FAT.

NO I WON'T. WHO CARES ANYWAY. LEAVE ME ALONE - I'VE HAD ENOUGH LECTURES FOR ONE NIGHT.

MAYBE IF YOU SPENT LESS TIME WATCHING TV, AND MORE TIME WORKING, WE WOULDN'T HAVE TO KEEP AFTER YOU.

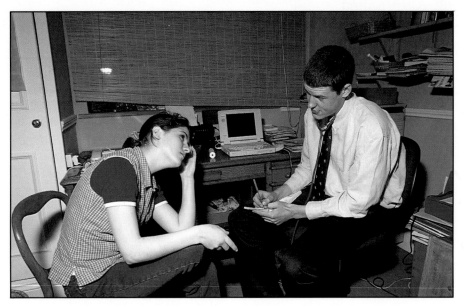

Mr. Summers has begun to believe that his family doesn't need him anymore. Sometimes depression may become so severe that people start to think their life is no longer worth living. Suicidal thoughts are a feature of depression for many. This is why it is so important to try to express feelings and not be afraid of seeking help with a problem. Some people have taken steps toward suicide – perhaps deciding on the method they will use – or have actually attempted it. Others have gone as far as to end their lives.

Most people are able to go through short periods of feeling down, and work through their feelings. Although this is described as being depressed, it is not the same as clinical depression, episodes of which can often last for several weeks at a time, and involve extremely severe mood swings. In some cases, clinical depression can result in changes in someone's personality. This kind of depression can't be solved by trying to cheer someone up. It is an illness and sufferers may need special treatment and support to help them recover. This can also take time.

Everyone may feel depressed sometimes. They might not be clinically depressed. There may be other reasons for these symptoms. A correct diagnosis must be made, so that the proper support and treatment can be given.

CAUSES OF DEPRESSION

THE REASON FOR A PERSON BECOMING DEPRESSED WILL VARY FROM CASE TO CASE.

Nobody understands the exact causes of clinical depression, but there are many theories. It is likely to be the result of several factors acting together at the same time.

Anyone can suffer with depression. The numbers of young people with depression appear to be increasing. Research suggests that for some, depression could be an inherited condition – relatives of sufferers have been shown to be more at risk. This has not yet been proved. Other possible causes are disruption to the nerve patterns in the brain, or a hormone imbalance. Depression can come with some illnesses. Diet is thought by some to play a part – a lack of the correct vitamins and iron can lead to some of the symptoms. There are also social and psychological factors. A person mourning the loss or death of a loved one may go through a period of severe depression. Someone undergoing the stress of not having enough money to live on, or a relationship breaking up, may also become depressed.

Big changes in life, such as moving or changing schools, can be a cause of depression for some people.

▽ Six weeks later, Ian and Alan were hurrying to get to class.

▽ Danny and Gary just laughed and pushed past them.

> HEY! WATCH WHERE YOU'RE GOING, FOUR EYES.

> HE CAN'T! LOOK AT THE GLASSES. HE PROBABLY NEEDS SONAR TO FIND HIS WAY AROUND.

> VERY FUNNY GARY. ANYWAY, YOU WALKED INTO ME. MAYBE YOU NEED GLASSES TOO!

> WHAT IS IT WITH DANNY?

> I DON'T KNOW. HE USED TO BE OKAY. YOU WANT TO BE CAREFUL AROUND HIM. I'VE HEARD HE CAN BE NASTY IF YOU CROSS HIM.

▽ The next day, Ian arrived at school to find the others discussing Ricky.

> IAN, DID YOU HEAR? RICKY'S PARENTS ARE SPLITTING UP.

> WHAT? HOW DO YOU KNOW?

> I WENT TO HIS HOUSE LAST NIGHT. HIS DAD'S MOVED OUT ALREADY. HE WAS REALLY UPSET ABOUT IT.

> SO WOULD YOU BE IF IT WERE YOUR PARENTS. MINE DIVORCED TWO YEARS AGO. IT WAS AWFUL.

> I REMEMBER. YOU WERE LIKE A DIFFERENT PERSON AT THE TIME.

> I CAN'T IMAGINE HOW I'D FEEL IF MY MOM AND DAD SEPARATED. POOR RICKY.

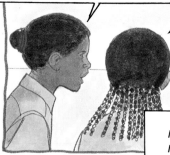

▽ On the way home, Deepak noticed Ian was very quiet.

> I WAS JUST THINKING ABOUT DAD. IT MAKES ME ANGRY TO SEE HIM. HE'S CHANGED, AND HE LOOKS SO DEPRESSED.

> LOSING YOUR JOB AND HAVING YOUR HOME REPOSSESSED IS ENOUGH TO MAKE ANYONE DEPRESSED.

> I MEAN, IT'S SUPPOSED TO BE A HAPPY OCCASION, BUT MOM COULDN'T COPE AT ALL. SHE KEPT CRYING ALL THE TIME.

> LOTS OF THINGS CAN. AFTER MY SISTER WAS BORN, MY MOM GOT REALLY STRANGE.

> THAT'S HOW IT IS WITH DAD. IT'S AS IF WHAT'S HAPPENED HAS MADE HIM GIVE UP HOPE.

△ Ian said goodbye to the others and hurried home.

Growing up, many young people have to deal with significant life changes. Some have had to face the break-up of their parents' relationship, or get used to being part of a stepfamily. Others have gone through problems with friendships or bullying, or been worried about going to a new school. If you haven't chosen the change yourself, the feelings you have about it may be more difficult to cope with than if you have, but you can learn to handle them. The first step is to admit that you have these emotions and talk to someone who can help you deal with them.

Ian thinks his dad has given up hope. Having too much or too little pressure can be harmful. Thinking that you cannot cope can sometimes be a factor in depression. If you believe the pressure you are under is getting out of hand, talk to someone you trust about your feelings. Many young people often wrongly think that they are the only ones who feel a certain way. Talking can help them to realize that everyone experiences difficult emotions at times, and that there are ways of handling these.

Most parents are happy at the birth of their new baby. Some, like Deepak's mom, find their feelings are the opposite. Many experience a period of depression – known as postnatal depression. This might be caused by high levels of certain hormones in the body. Postnatal depression can be severe, but most people are able to recover with support and counseling.

OTHER MENTAL HEALTH PROBLEMS

JUST AS EVERY PERSON IS PHYSICALLY DIFFERENT FROM EVERYONE ELSE, NO TWO PEOPLE'S MINDS WORK IN EXACTLY THE SAME WAY.

Despite this, many people are afraid of difference. This often makes understanding mental health problems harder.

Mental distress happens for a variety of reasons and affects people in different ways. Some are born with a particular condition. Others might develop a problem as the result of injury or disease, or because of a specific stressful life event. Of course, events themselves do not directly cause a problem. However, people can be so deeply affected by what has happened, that they are unable to deal effectively with their thoughts and feelings. Some people are able to express themselves easily. Others find it difficult to show emotion, and may bottle things up, which can lead to problems in some cases. Those with some kinds of mental distress are often seen as lacking in intelligence. But we all have different mental capacities. Your friends may be better at certain subjects than you are, and vice versa. The assumptions people make about mental illness are often misguided, or actually wrong, and only get in the way of understanding the subject.

People in mental distress may find it difficult to cope with tasks and situations others take for granted.

▽ When he got home, Ian was surprised to find his Uncle Max there.

YOUR UNCLE'S BEEN TO SEE YOUR DAD. HE'S GIVEN HIM SOMETHING TO HELP HIM SLEEP.

WHY? I'D HAVE THOUGHT THAT'S THE LAST THING HE NEEDS.

YOU DON'T UNDERSTAND, IAN. I KNOW YOU'RE ANGRY, BUT I THINK YOUR DAD'S REALLY QUITE ILL.

▽ Mrs. Summers was upset. Max tried to explain to Ian.

YOUR DAD'S DEPRESSION ISN'T LIKE WE ALL GET FROM TIME TO TIME. I THINK HE'S GOING TO NEED A GREAT DEAL OF HELP AND SUPPORT TO GET THROUGH THIS.

BUT HOW CAN WE HELP HIM? IT'S STILL ALL IN HIS MIND, ISN'T IT?

AT YOUR AGE YOU'RE PROBABLY USED TO EXPERIENCING MOOD SWINGS. MOST OF US GET USED TO HANDLING DIFFICULT FEELINGS AS WE GROW UP. BUT FOR SOME IT CAN GET BEYOND THEIR CONTROL. MENTAL ILLNESS NEEDS PROPER TREATMENT, JUST LIKE PHYSICAL ILLNESS DOES.

◁ Max said there was still a lot to understand about the way the mind worked.

WILL HE BE LIKE GREAT-GRANDMA? SHE WAS FUNNY – SHE'D TELL ME THINGS SHE DID AT MY AGE, THEN SHE COULDN'T REMEMBER WHO I WAS.

THERE ARE ALL KINDS OF THINGS THAT CAN AFFECT THE WAY THE MIND WORKS, IAN.

YOUR GREAT GRANDMA HAD ALZHEIMER'S DISEASE, DARLING. THIS ISN'T THE SAME.

▷ Ian hadn't thought of his dad as mentally ill.
▽ The La Salles were eating dinner.

YOU DON'T LOOK WELL, TRISHA. IF YOU HADN'T SUCH A HEALTHY APPETITE I'D THINK YOU WERE COMING DOWN WITH SOMETHING.

I'M OKAY. MAY I BE EXCUSED? I'VE GOT WORK TO DO.

▽ Trisha went upstairs. Later on, Alan went into her room.

TRISH, ARE YOU ALL RIGHT? I THOUGHT I HEARD YOU GETTING SICK EARLIER.

I MUST HAVE EATEN SOMETHING THAT DISAGREED WITH ME. DON'T WORRY, I'LL BE FINE.

Alzheimer's Disease (pronounced Alts-high-mers) & Dementia • These usually affect people in old age, involving the progressive deterioration of memory and mental functions. As the conditions become worse, a person may have personality changes, have difficulty speaking or recognizing people, and become dependent upon others to care for them. There is no cure, but the percentage of older people affected is still quite small.

Breakdown, nervous • This is a term that is used to describe an emotional overload, which stops a person from functioning normally. A breakdown might be the result of a traumatic event, or be caused by too much stress. It can turn into depression. Many people who have a nervous breakdown recover.

Delusion • A delusion is a belief or idea which a person holds onto, despite proof that it is not true. Someone who suffers with delusions might have difficulty recognizing and understanding what is real and what isn't.

Eating disorders • Although eating disorders have a physical effect, they are usually the result of emotional problems. People suffering from Anorexia Nervosa will starve themselves, may lose huge amounts of weight yet be unable to see themselves as thin. Those with Bulimia Nervosa may also go through periods of starvation, but will also binge on large amounts of food, then make themselves sick to get rid of it.

Manic depression • People with manic depression will have all the symptoms of depression, but they will also have great highs. They will have extreme feelings of excitement or recklessness. They may become hyperactive – doing several things at once. The period of "mania"

might change to the other extreme of gloom.

Obsession • An obsession is an intense interest in or preoccupation with a person or subject. Sometimes it can seem

to be the only thing that matters in your life. Some young people become obsessed with the way they look. If they have pimples, for instance, they feel that this makes them less attractive as a person, which isn't true.

Paranoia (para-noy-a) • This is another kind of mental disorder, in which a person falsely thinks that, for instance, they are being persecuted or targeted by others – perhaps people they can't see.

Phobia (fo-bee-a) • A phobia is an intense fear of a specific object, activity, or situation. Often the cause of a phobia is something like closed spaces, water, or spiders. The fear is only a phobia if it becomes a real source of distress.

Psychosis (sigh-ko-sis) • Psychosis is a mental disorder, in which people lose all sense of reality. There are many psychotic

disorders. Psychosis can be dangerous, if people have no sense of right and wrong.

Schizophrenia (skitso-free-nia) • People with schizophrenia are often wrongly described as having a split personality. In fact, it is a problem of the thinking processes. It is a psychotic disorder, and people might have difficulty focusing on what is

real. Some people may need hospitalization. Drugs can stabilize the condition.

Self-harm • Some people with mental or emotional problems deliberately hurt themselves. Some, for instance, have cut or burned their skin. Many sufferers feel that they are worthless or deserve to be in pain. People can be helped to stop.

Shyness, anxiety, and panic attacks • Many young people are shy. It can be an upsetting emotion, but one which can be worked on. Anxiety and panic can stop one from functioning normally in situations where one would usually be able to control. In some cases, this can become extreme. Panic attacks might be accompanied by dizziness, chest pain, and sweating. With help many people come to terms with the causes of their panic.

EFFECTS ON PEOPLES LIVES

THE EXTENT TO WHICH SOMEONE'S LIFE IS AFFECTED BY A MENTAL PROBLEM WILL DEPEND ON THE PERSON AND CONDITION INVOLVED.

The severity of the condition, the support and treatment someone receives, and the response of the person to the problem all play a part. Some of the effects might include inability to concentrate, or a lack of motivation to do normal day-to-day activities. This might lead to neglect, both of self and of others.

Some people experience a loss of appetite, or a change in their sleep patterns. They might go through changes in their personality, perhaps becoming rude, even violent, toward others. Some might try to hurt themselves. Or they might have periods where their memory is affected, or what they say doesn't make sense to other people. For young people, their schoolwork might suffer. Other people might make cruel remarks because of their situation. For adults, mental distress may cause problems with employment. Often sufferers find it difficult to find work, because of companies' attitudes toward mental distress. Some people are so severely affected that they need constant care and attention.

Mental health problems can often place a lot of strain on relationships with friends and family.

▽ Three weeks later, Nadine, Lisa, and Trisha had arranged to meet in town.

LET'S GET SOMETHING TO EAT FIRST. I'M STARVING.

I'M NOT HUNGRY. I HAD A BIG BREAKFAST.

WELL IT DOESN'T LOOK LIKE IT. YOU'RE AS THIN AS A RAKE. HAVE YOU LOST MORE WEIGHT?

A COUPLE OF POUNDS. I NEEDED TO. I LOOKED AWFUL.

DON'T BE STUPID. YOU LOOKED GREAT.

YOU SURE DID. YOU WANT TO BE CAREFUL YOU DON'T LOSE TOO MUCH.

△ Trisha suddenly said she'd changed her mind about shopping, and left.

▽ At school the next day, Nadine went to look for Alan.

IS SOMETHING GOING ON AT HOME? TRISHA'S ACTING VERY STRANGELY LATELY. SHE WON'T TALK TO ME OR LISA.

I DON'T KNOW. I'M WORRIED TOO. I THINK SHE'S WORRIED ABOUT THE EXAMS NEXT MONTH.

▽ Meanwhile, Ricky was talking to Ian.

IT'S DEFINITE THAT THEY'RE GETTING A DIVORCE. THEY'RE TALKING ABOUT SELLING THE HOUSE. I MIGHT HAVE TO GO TO A NEW SCHOOL.

LOOK, GUYS, I THINK THE LITTLE BOY'S GOING TO CRY.

LEAVE HIM ALONE, CAN'T YOU. WHY DO YOU HAVE TO BE SO HORRIBLE?

◁ Danny ran off laughing. Ian was miserable the rest of the day.

DO YOU KNOW WHO YOU'RE TALKING TO? OR HAVE YOU LOST YOUR MIND LIKE YOUR FATHER?

GET OFF ME! YOU DON'T KNOW WHAT YOU'RE TALKING ABOUT.

EVERYONE KNOWS YOUR DAD'S A WEIRDO!

WHAT'S GOING ON? WHAT'S WRONG WITH DAD?

I JUST GOT IN, AND FOUND HIM LIKE THAT. I'M CALLING AN AMBULANCE. I THINK HE MIGHT HAVE TAKEN SOME PILLS.

Some people have a bad attitude toward mental distress.
Danny is being unkind. This sort of reaction can make people afraid of admitting to having a problem, or of others finding out about a friend or relative with one. They might be worried about what the response will be. Mental distress is not something anyone should be ashamed of, and not a subject to make fun of. Slang words describing those with different mental health problems can be very hurtful.

Some people look after relatives on a constant basis.
Children and young people may also find themselves with this role. It can take a lot of time and energy. It is vital that the guardian's concerns and worries, and his or her own needs are taken into consideration. Otherwise the pressure could lead to problems for the guardian.

Ricky and Ian are both miserable about the situation with their parents.
As well as the effects on the sufferer, mental health problems can also affect the people she or he is closest to. It can be very hard to see those you care about suffering. It can be exasperating too, for instance with depression, if you yourself can see no reason for a person being depressed. You might be angry at that person. Such feelings are natural, but they won't help.

STRESS AND MENTAL HEALTH

IT WOULD BE IMPOSSIBLE TO AVOID SOME STRESS IN OUR LIVES. IT CAN EVEN BE BENEFICIAL IF IT IS REASONABLE AND MANAGEABLE.

Too much stress is harmful and stops people from functioning properly. In some cases it can lead to other mental health problems. Research suggests that more and more young people are experiencing periods of increased stress. Sometimes this is caused by pressure at home – perhaps because of problems within the family, such as the break-up of their parents' relationship, or because of other people's expectations of them. Going to a new school, worrying about exams, or making friends can also all cause stress. Many young people often face a lack of opportunity as they grow up – perhaps in terms of the social activity offered or the employment they will be able to go into. Boredom and uncertainty about the future can all cause anxiety and put young people under pressure. Many develop their own ways of handling stress – for instance socializing, music, dancing, or sports. It's a matter of finding out what works for you. If you are under stress, it is important to talk to someone about it.

Exams are very trying times for many young people. While some can take them in their stride, others become very anxious about them.

21

▽ Ian's dad was in the hospital. He had nearly died from an overdose.

WHY WOULD HE DO SOMETHING LIKE THAT?

I DON'T KNOW DARLING. WHAT HAPPENS NOW, MAX?

ONCE WE'RE SURE HE'S OUT OF DANGER, I'LL HAVE HIM ADMITTED TO A SPECIAL UNIT FOR A WHILE, SO HE CAN GET THE SUPPORT HE NEEDS.

▽ The two of them ran off quickly. Danny was too shocked to chase them.

WHERE DID YOU HEAR THAT ABOUT DANNY'S FATHER?

I SAW THEM TOGETHER ONCE. YOU SHOULD HAVE SEEN THE WAY HE TREATED DANNY. IT WAS AWFUL. DANNY LOOKED REALLY SCARED OF HIM.

▽ A few weeks later, it was time for Trisha's exams.

THERE YOU ARE. HOW COME YOU LEFT EARLY THIS MORNING? MOM AND DAD WERE LOOKING FOR YOU.

SO THEY COULD TELL ME YET AGAIN THAT I HAVE TO DO WELL?

TRISHA, WHY ARE YOU DOING THIS TO YOURSELF? YOU LOOK TERRIBLE. WHY WON'T YOU TALK TO US? WE COULD HELP.

▽ A few days later in town, Deepak and Ian ran into Danny again.

UH, OH, TROUBLE. AND IT LOOKS LIKE HE'S BEEN DRINKING.

HEY, FOUR EYES. I HEARD THEY FINALLY LOCKED YOUR DAD UP.

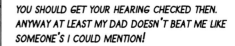

YOU SHOULD GET YOUR HEARING CHECKED THEN. ANYWAY AT LEAST MY DAD DOESN'T BEAT ME LIKE SOMEONE'S I COULD MENTION!

WELL I WOULDN'T WANT TO BE YOU TOMORROW AT SCHOOL. STILL HE SHOULDN'T HAVE SAID THOSE THINGS ABOUT YOUR DAD.

I DIDN'T WANT ANYONE TO KNOW HE WAS IN THE HOSPITAL AT FIRST. THEN SOMEONE OVERHEARD ME TALKING TO MOM ABOUT VISITING. IT'S OKAY NOW. MOST PEOPLE ARE FINE.

NO YOU COULDN'T. YOU DON'T UNDERSTAND. EVERYONE THINKS THEY CAN TELL ME WHAT TO DO. WELL I'M SICK OF IT. I DON'T CARE ABOUT THE STUPID EXAMS!

△ With that, she turned around and ran back out of school before the others could stop her.

The stress of being bullied can be very intense indeed.
Bullies like Danny rely on causing fear and upset in other people. Nobody should have to put up with being bullied, and you should try never to go along with it. Telling someone might be difficult, but many bullies need help themselves.

Abuse can be a factor in some cases of depression and mental distress.
The number of reports of physical or sexual abuse seems to have increased in recent years. Many young people wrongly believe the abuse is in some way their own fault. Their abuser may even tell them this to try to make them afraid of telling anyone what happened. But this is not true. All children and young people have the right to grow up protected, and to feel free to discuss their problems. Abuse should always be reported, no matter who is doing the abusing.

Many young people want to try new things and have new experiences.
Some, like Danny, have experimented with drugs and alcohol, either because they think it is a grown-up thing to do, or because they believe it will give them a release from what they see as the boredom of their everyday lives. However, alcohol and drugs don't provide solutions to worries or problems. In fact, far from being an escape from distress or unhappiness, alcohol and drugs can actually cause problems, make existing ones worse, and be a threat to both your physical and mental health.

WHAT HELP IS AVAILABLE ?

THERE ARE MANY DIFFERENT KINDS OF HELP AVAILABLE TO PEOPLE WITH SOME FORM OF MENTAL HEALTH PROBLEM.

What is appropriate for one person might not always be right for someone else, even if the condition seems to be the same.
Treatment must be suited to both the distress and the individual. Drugs are used to treat some illnesses. In most cases drugs only control the symptoms of the condition, they don't cure it. There are specially trained people – such as psychiatrists, psychologists, and counselors – who can offer help. They will try to get to the cause of the distress and help the sufferer. In some cases, people may need to spend time in the hospital. Getting better can take a long time for many people, and some may never recover fully.

Self-help groups can assist those with the same kinds of problems to share and discuss their feelings.

▽ Later, Mr. & Mrs. La Salle tried to talk to Trisha.

TRISHA, WHAT ARE YOU DOING? THE SCHOOL SAID YOU DIDN'T TURN UP FOR EXAMS TODAY.

SO WHAT? I FIGURED IF I DON'T DO THEM AT ALL, THEN YOU WON'T BE DISAPPOINTED WHEN I DON'T DO AS WELL AS YOU WANT.

TRISHA THAT'S RIDICULOUS.

NO IT'S NOT. EXCUSE ME - I THINK I'M GOING TO BE SICK.

TRISHA COME BACK - WHY ARE YOU DOING THIS TO YOURSELF?

LEAVE HER, LOVE. I THINK MAYBE WE SHOULD CALL A DOCTOR.

△ Mr. La Salle had realized that Trisha had a serious problem.

▽ A few days later, Ian and his mom were visiting his dad.

MAX SAYS HE THINKS YOU'LL BE COMING HOME SOON.

I'M SORRY ABOUT THE THINGS I SAID, DAD. I JUST THOUGHT YOU NEEDED TO SNAP OUT OF IT. UNCLE MAX TALKED TO ME ABOUT IT ALL, AND I KNOW HOW WRONG I WAS ABOUT YOU.

IT'S SO DIFFICULT TO DESCRIBE HOW IT FEELS. IT'S LIKE NOTHING MATTERS - AS THOUGH SOMETHING IS CONTROLLING YOU, GRADUALLY DRAINING ALL YOUR ENERGY. IT WAS HARD AT FIRST, BUT TALKING TO A PSYCHIATRIST HAS REALLY HELPED ME.

▽ The next day at school, Ian and Ricky saw that Alan and Nadine looked upset.

▽ Nadine explained that the doctors thought Trisha had bulimia.

IT'S TRISHA. SHE'S ILL, AND I THINK IT'S MY FAULT. I'D SEEN HER GETTING SICK BEFORE, AND I SHOULD HAVE REALIZED WHAT WAS HAPPENING.

THAT'S NOT TRUE. PEOPLE CAN BE VERY CLEVER AT HIDING THE TRUTH. I'D NOTICED HER LOSING WEIGHT MYSELF.

IT'S AN EATING DISORDER.

I KNOW WHAT IT IS. BUT WHY TRISHA?

I THINK IT'S BECAUSE OF MOM AND DAD PUTTING SO MUCH PRESSURE ON HER ABOUT SCHOOL AND STUFF.

TRISHA HASN'T SAID MUCH YET. BUT THE DOCTOR SAID IT ISN'T ONLY ABOUT FOOD - IT'S ABOUT THE WAY SHE FEELS ABOUT HERSELF.

WHY? WHAT'S WRONG WITH HER?

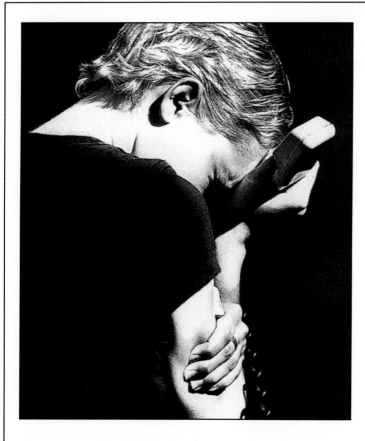

Ian now understands the seriousness of his dad's depression.
With illnesses such as this, it can be tempting simply to tell people to "cheer up," or to emphasize the good things about the person's life. It's natural to want to try to help and to think that focusing on positive things is the first step in dealing with the emotions. This might be useful with the kind of depression we all experience from time to time. However, most people who suffer with clinical depression will tell you that this approach does no good. While they are depressed, many refuse to believe that anything in their lives is worthwhile.

Trisha's friends feel upset at not having noticed her problem earlier.
Mental distress is a part of life. One of the ways people can help is by being more aware of mental health as an important issue, and not viewing illness as though it is something weird or dangerous. People who are affected have the right to be treated with the same respect as everyone else, and have their needs met.

Mr. Summers was reluctant at first to seek help with his problem.
Some people who don't think twice about visiting their doctor dislike the idea of seeing a psychiatrist, specialist, or phoning a helpline. There is nothing shameful or suspicious about therapy and sharing problems. Psychiatrists are only doctors who specialize in treating mental as well as physical illness.

LOOKING AFTER YOURSELF

GROWING UP CAN BE AN EXCITING EXPERIENCE. BUT IT DOES PRESENT CHALLENGES TO YOUNG PEOPLE.

Your emotional well-being is important, particularly during puberty, when the changes you go through may make you vulnerable.
Having a strong sense of self-esteem – a belief in your own worth – can help you to avoid all kinds of problems. People who are aware of their feelings, including the bad ones, and can express them honestly and appropriately are likely to be more emotionally healthy than those who bottle things up. You should never ignore a possible problem. Thinking something will just go away can often make things worse. Looking for solutions, and trying to focus on positive issues is important. Taking care of your physical health, by eating a balanced diet, getting plenty of exercise, and having relaxation time, can all help to strengthen your emotional well-being and make you feel good about yourself.

Looking after your emotional health is just as important as taking care of yourself physically.

▽ It was two months later. Ian's friends had come over to the house for his birthday.

THANKS, RICKY. HOW ARE THINGS?

OK, I SUPPOSE. I'M GOING TO BE MOVING AS SOON AS THE HOUSE HAS BEEN SOLD, BUT I'LL STILL BE GOING TO THE SAME SCHOOL.

YOU SEEM TO BE TAKING THINGS PRETTY CALMLY.

I WAS UPSET AT FIRST - LIKE WHEN MOM AND DAD FIRST SPLIT UP. BUT WE'VE TALKED ABOUT IT A LOT, AND I FEEL OKAY NOW.

IAN, YOUR DAD'S ASKING FOR YOU. HOW'S HE GETTING ALONG?

HE'S STILL GOING TO COUNSELING, BUT THINGS ARE MUCH BETTER NOW. NO NEWS OF A JOB YET, THOUGH, BUT HE HAS STARTED LOOKING AGAIN. HOW'S TRISHA? I WISH SHE COULD HAVE COME.

▽ Alan told them Trisha went to a group twice a week to talk about her problem.

SHE'S STILL VERY THIN, THOUGH, ISN'T SHE.

OF COURSE SHE IS. YOU CAN'T JUST FORCE PEOPLE TO EAT - IT'S NOT AS SIMPLE AS THAT.

I STILL WISH WE'D REALIZED EARLIER WHAT WAS GOING ON. MOM AND DAD HAVE BEEN GREAT, THOUGH.

HEY, THERE SHE IS. TRISHA, I'M REALLY GLAD YOU COULD MAKE IT!

THANKS. I WASN'T GOING TO AT FIRST. BUT I JUST HEARD THAT I'M GOING TO BE ALLOWED TO SIT FOR MY EXAMS AGAIN NEXT SEMESTER. I CAN'T FIGURE OUT IF I'M EXCITED OR TERRIFIED!

DON'T BE EITHER! JUST TAKE THEM AS THEY COME.

IAN, I FORGOT TO TELL YOU. I RAN INTO DANNY YESTERDAY, AND HE WAS NICE TO ME!

I DON'T THINK HE WANTS TO BE A BULLY. HE JUST TAKES OUT HIS FEELINGS ABOUT HIMSELF ON OTHERS. IT'S SAD, REALLY.

I DON'T BELIEVE IT. DANNY BEING NICE TO PEOPLE - NOW ALL WE NEED IS A CURE FOR ACNE AND WE'LL ALL BE OKAY. RIGHT, LISA?

△ Lisa picked up a piece of ice and slipped it down Ricky's back!

Bottling up emotions, or brooding, can sometimes lead to problems.
Instead of being a minor emotional difficulty, the situation can grow out of all proportion. Some feelings can be quickly dealt with – maybe by having a good cry, or going for a long walk to calm down.
It is important to be prepared for uncomfortable feelings. They are a natural part of life, and it would be impossible to avoid them all. Pretending you don't have a particular emotion will not help to work it through.

Ricky has discussed the situation with his parents and it has helped him come to terms with it.
Depression and other mental health problems are not something to be ashamed of. If you are having emotional problems, or are under a lot of stress, talking to someone you trust can help. You might want to practice what you want to say first, so that your concerns are clear. The person you choose could be a friend, a member of the family, or an outside agency.

Trisha is glad that she is getting help with her bulimia.
With many mental health problems, it's often also up to the sufferer to recognize that the problem exists, and to want to be helped. This may not always be easy. However, as with most difficulties, the earlier you address it, the easier it is likely to be to find a solution. At the same time, it is never too late to seek help.

WHAT CAN WE DO?

HAVING READ THIS BOOK, YOU SHOULD UNDERSTAND MORE ABOUT DEPRESSION AND OTHER MENTAL HEALTH PROBLEMS.

You will know how important it is to take care of your emotional well-being, and that mental distress is not something to be afraid or ashamed of.

You might also want to find out more about different mental health issues, so that you know the facts, and can challenge prejudice and discrimination. Not everyone will come into contact with mental illness or develop a problem. However, situations that will make emotional demands on you, and put you under some stress, are an unavoidable part of life. Learning how to cope with these is important. If you believe you have a problem, or are concerned about someone else, discussing the matter with another person, such as a friend, relative, or perhaps your family doctor might help.

National Alliance For the Mentally Ill
200 N. Glebe Road, Suite 1015
Arlington, VA 22203-3754
800-950-6264

National Mental Health Association
1021 Prince Street
Alexandria, VA 22314-2971
800-969-NMHA

National Council on Child Abuse and Family Violence
1155 Connecticut Avenue, NW,
Suite 400
Washington, DC 20036
800-222-2000

ADULTS CAN HELP TOO, BY REMEMBERING THAT THEIR ATTITUDE TOWARD MENTAL HEALTH ISSUES CAN INFLUENCE THEIR CHILDREN'S VIEWS.

Young people often also look to adults to be there for them to approach with worries and concerns that they want to discuss. Adults and young people who have read this book together may find it useful to share their thoughts and ideas about the issues raised. Some people who would like advice about aspects of mental health might prefer to talk to someone not directly involved. Information, help, and support can be obtained from the organizations listed below.

Child Quest International
1625 The Alameda,
Suite 400
San Jose, CA 95126
800-248-8020

Division For Physical and Health Disabilities
1920 Association Drive
Reston, VA 20191
763-620-3660

National Foundation For Depressive Illness
P.O. Box 2257
New York, NY 10116
800-248-4344

Al-Anon Family Group Headquarters
1600 Corporate
Landing Parkway
Virginia Beach, VA 23454
800-356-9996

National Alliance For Research For Schizophrenia and Depression
60 Cutter Mill Road,
Suite 404
Great Neck,
NY 11021-3196
800-829-8289

Institute For the Development of Emotional and Life Skills
4400 East-West Hwy.,
Suite 28
Bethesda, MD 20814
301-986-1479

Depressive and Manic Depressive Association
730 North Franklin,
Suite 501
Chicago, IL 60610
800-826-3632

INDEX

Photocredits

All the pictures in this book are by Roger Vlitos apart from pages: 20b: Jo Partridge/Help the Aged; 26t: The Samaritans.